Collins

Primary Social Studies for Antigua and Barbuda

STUDENT'S BOOK
GRADE 4

T0312375

Anthea S Thomas

William Collins' dream of knowledge for all began with the publication of his first book in 1819.

A self-educated mill worker, he not only enriched millions of lives, but also founded a flourishing publishing house. Today, staying true to this spirit, Collins books are packed with inspiration, innovation and practical expertise. They place you at the centre of a world of possibility and give you exactly what you need to explore it.

Collins. Freedom to teach.

Published by Collins
An imprint of HarperCollins*Publishers*
The News Building
1 London Bridge Street
London
SE1 9GF

HarperCollins Publishers
Macken House, 39/40 Mayor Street Upper,
Dublin 1, D01 C9W8, Ireland

Browse the complete Collins catalogue at
www.collins.co.uk

© HarperCollins*Publishers* Limited 2019
Maps © Collins Bartholomew Limited 2019, unless otherwise stated

10 9 8 7 6

ISBN 978-0-00-832492-6

British Library Cataloguing-in-Publication Data
A catalogue record for this publication is available from the British Library.

Author: Anthea S. Thomas
Commissioning editor: Elaine Higgleton
Development editor: Bruce Nicholson
In-house editors: Caroline Green, Alexandra Wells, Holly Woolnough
Copy editor: Sue Chapple
Proof reader: Jan Schubert
Cover designers: Kevin Robbins and Gordon MacGilp
Cover image: Maquiladora/Shutterstock
Typesetter: QBS
Illustrators: QBS and Ann Paganuzzi
Production controller: Sarah Burke
Printed and bound in the UK by Ashford Colour Press Ltd.

Acknowledgements

The publishers wish to thank the following for permission to reproduce photographs. Every effort has been made to trace copyright holders and to obtain their permission for the use of copyright materials. The publishers will gladly receive any information enabling them to rectify any error or omission at the first opportunity.
(t = top, c = centre, b = bottom, l = left, r = right)

p29 Sean Pavone/Shutterstock; p30 Leonard Zhukovsky/Shutterstock; p31 Art Directors & TRIP/Alamy Stock Photo; p32 Evenfh/Shutterstock; p33 Sarah Cheriton-Jones/Shutterstock; p34 Mbrand85/Shutterstock; p36l Travelview/Shutterstock; p36r Underworld/Shutterstock; p37t Lunamarina/Shutterstock; p37b G-stockstudio/Shutterstock; p38t Parmna/Shutterstock; p38b Okcm/Shutterstock; p41 World History Archive/Alamy Stock Photo; p42t Marina Movschowitz/Alamy Stock Photo; p42b ImageBROKER/Alamy Stock Photo; p43l Marekuliasz/Shutterstock; p43r Pascal Lagesse/Shutterstock; p44 The Print Collector/Alamy Stock Photo; p45 Jeep2499/Shutterstock; p47 North Wind Picture Archives/Alamy Stock Photo; p50l Xshot/Shutterstock; p50r Uwe Kreth/Shutterstock; p51 John Warburton-Lee Photography/Alamy Stock Photo; p52 Richard Whitcombe/Shutterstock; p54 Juneisy Q. Hawkins/Shutterstock; p55 Altin Osmanaj/Shutterstock; p56 Ramunas Bruzas/Shutterstock; p57 Delray Beach Photog/Shutterstock; p58 Janos Rautonen/Shutterstock; p59l PHB.cz (Richard Semik)/Shutterstock; p59r Gem Russan/Shutterstock; p60l Straga/Shutterstock; p60r IS2010-02/Alamy Stock Photo; p61l Karen Hadley/Shutterstock; p61r Prometheus72/Shutterstock; p62 Kletr/Shutterstock; p63 Meryll/Shutterstock; p64 Papakah/Shutterstock; p65 Pix/Alamy Stock Photo; p66 Dbimages/Alamy Stock Photo; p67 Fasttailwind/Shutterstock; p71 Ethan Daniels/Shutterstock; p72 Robert_s/Shutterstock; p74 NG Images/Alamy Stock Photo; p76 Tad Denson/Shutterstock; p80 Designua/Shutterstock; p81t Ioat/Shutterstock; p82 Travel and Learn/Shutterstock; p83 Sean Pavone/Shutterstock; p84 Simon Dabbhauer/Shutterstock; p85 Stuart Hunter/Alamy Stock Photo; p87 Mark Pearson/Alamy Stock Photo; p88t Xfilephotos/Shutterstock; p88b R_Tee/Shutterstock; p89 With thanks to the National Office of Disaster Services; p90 Agencja Fotograficzna Caro/Alamy Stock Photo; p91l BATMANV/Shutterstock; p91r WeStudio/Shutterstock; p92 Lorna Roberts/Shutterstock; p93 Kallayanee Naloka/Shutterstock; p94tl Sergiy Kuzmin/Shutterstock; p94tr Mark Summerfield/Alamy Stock Photo; p94bl Findlay/Alamy Stock Photo; p94br Terry Harris/Alamy Stock Photo; p96 Iurii Kachkovskyi/Shutterstock; p97 Iofoto/Shutterstock; p98 StockLite/Shutterstock; p101 Jenny Matthews/Alamy Stock Photo; p102 Wavebreakmedia/Shutterstock; p103 Michaeljung/Shutterstock; p105 Flamingo Images/Shutterstock; p106 Toy-Ting/Shutterstock; p108 Voyagerix/Shutterstock; p109 Sergio Stakhnyk/Shutterstock; p110t Kitch Bain/Shutterstock, p110b Sheila Fitzgerald/Shutterstock; p112 Stuar/Shutterstock; p113 PACIFIC PRESS/Alamy Stock Photo; p115l Photka/Shutterstock; p115r Nortongo/Shutterstock; p116 Leonard Zhukovsky/Shutterstock.

Contents

1 The Caribbean region

We are learning to:

- locate the Caribbean region in relation to the rest of the world
- locate Antigua and Barbuda in the Caribbean
- name and locate the main groupings of Caribbean countries
- name and locate the seas and oceans of the Caribbean
- explain what a map is
- practise map-reading skills
- understand longitude and latitude, and the points of the compass.

The Caribbean region

The Caribbean region consists of the Caribbean Sea, its islands (most of which enclose the sea) and the surrounding coasts. It lies near the continents of North and South America and near the region that is called Central America.

Several mainland territories in North and South America, such as Venezuela, are also on the Caribbean Sea and are therefore considered to be part of the wider Caribbean region.

The islands of the Caribbean region are also known as the West Indies.

Where in the world is the Caribbean?

To find the Caribbean on a world map:

- Find the continents of North America and South America.
- Look at the narrow strip of land that joins the two continents (Central America).
- To the east you will see the Gulf of Mexico and the Caribbean Sea.

The Caribbean region is located in and around the Caribbean Sea. It is southeast of the Gulf of Mexico and North America, east of Central America and north of South America.

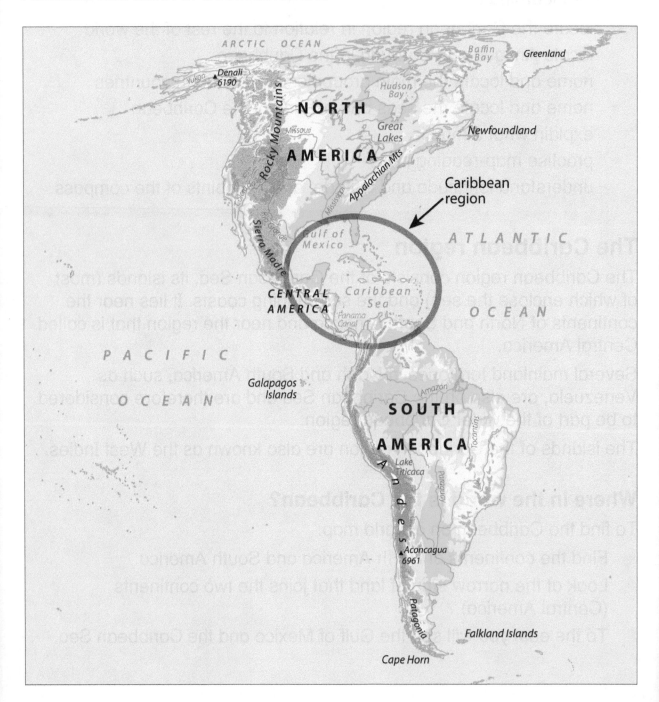

Locating Antigua and Barbuda

The map below shows the islands of the Caribbean in more detail.

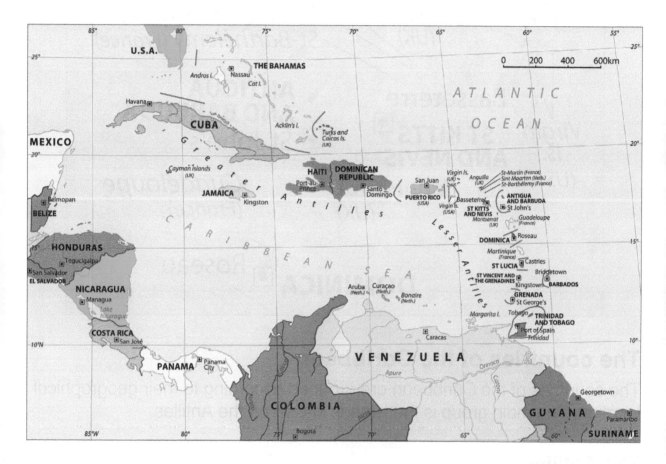

Antigua and Barbuda is in the east of the Caribbean Sea, north of Guadeloupe and southeast of Anguilla.

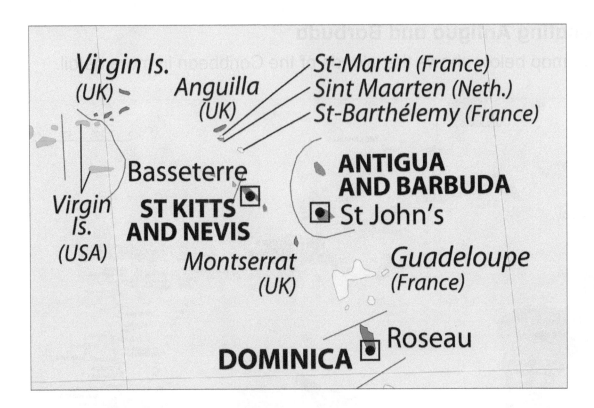

The countries of the Caribbean

The countries of the Caribbean are grouped according to their geographical location. The main group is the islands known as the Antilles.

The Antilles

A group of islands, such as those in the Caribbean region, is called an archipelago. The archipelago of the Antilles is divided into smaller chains of islands. These are:

- the Greater Antilles which bound the Caribbean Sea to the north
- the Lesser Antilles to the south and the east.

The Greater Antilles

There are five main islands in the Greater Antilles – Cuba, Hispaniola (Dominican Republic and Haiti), Puerto Rico, Jamaica and the Cayman Islands. The Greater Antilles makes up more than 90 per cent of the land area of the West Indies. These islands are also home to more than 90 per cent of the population of the West Indies.

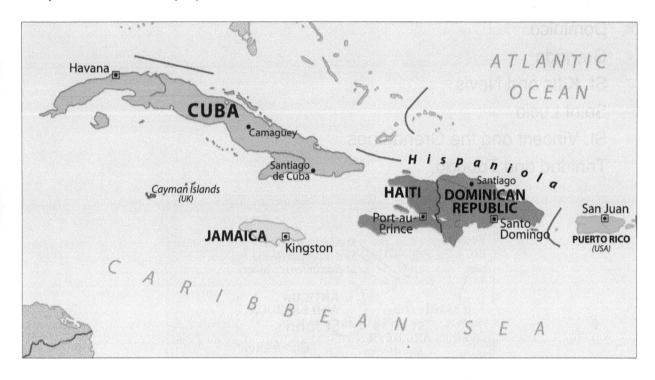

The Lesser Antilles

The islands of the Lesser Antilles tend to be much smaller. There are eight independent countries as well as sixteen other non-sovereign states and territories. The eight independent countries are:

- Antigua and Barbuda
- Barbados
- Dominica
- Grenada
- St. Kitts and Nevis
- Saint Lucia
- St. Vincent and the Grenadines
- Trinidad and Tobago.

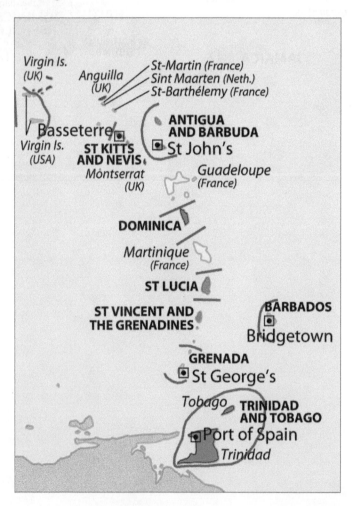

The islands of the Lesser Antilles are divided into:

- the Windward Islands in the south
- the Leeward Islands in the north
- the Leeward Antilles in the west.

The Windward Islands

The Windward Islands are the southern islands of the Lesser Antilles. They include:

- Dominica
- Martinique
- Saint Lucia
- St. Vincent and the Grenadines
- Grenada.

Barbados, and Trinidad and Tobago, are not really part of the Windward Islands, but are sometimes included in the group as they are near the other islands. Barbados is the most easterly Caribbean island.

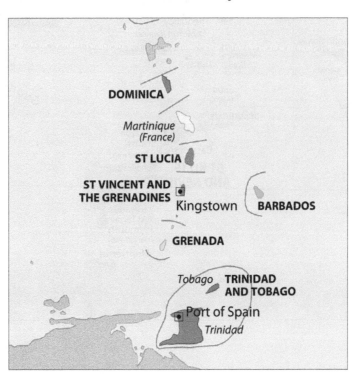

The Leeward Islands

The Leeward Islands are the northern islands of the Lesser Antilles chain, east of Puerto Rico and running south to Guadeloupe. They are situated where the northeastern Caribbean Sea meets the western Atlantic Ocean. They include:

- The British Virgin Islands
- Anguilla
- St. Kitts and Nevis
- Antigua and Barbuda
- Guadeloupe
- The US Virgin Islands
- Montserrat.

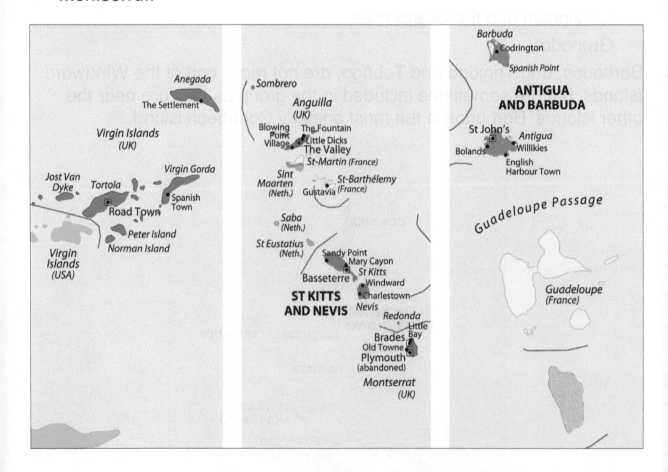

The Bahamas and Turks and Caicos

The Commonwealth of the Bahamas is a country consisting of 29 islands, 661 cays and 2387 islets (rocks). It is located in the Atlantic Ocean north of Cuba and Hispaniola, northwest of the Turks and Caicos Islands, and southeast of Florida in the United States. It lies to the north of the Greater Antilles.

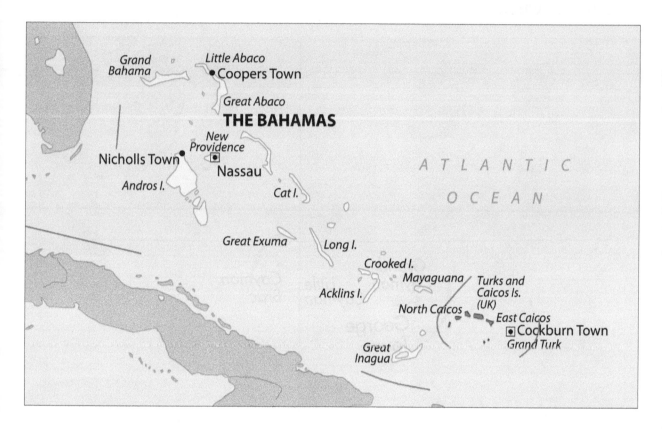

Cayman Islands

The Cayman Islands is a British Overseas Territory located in the western Caribbean Sea. The territory is made up of three islands:

- Grand Cayman
- Cayman Brac
- Little Cayman.

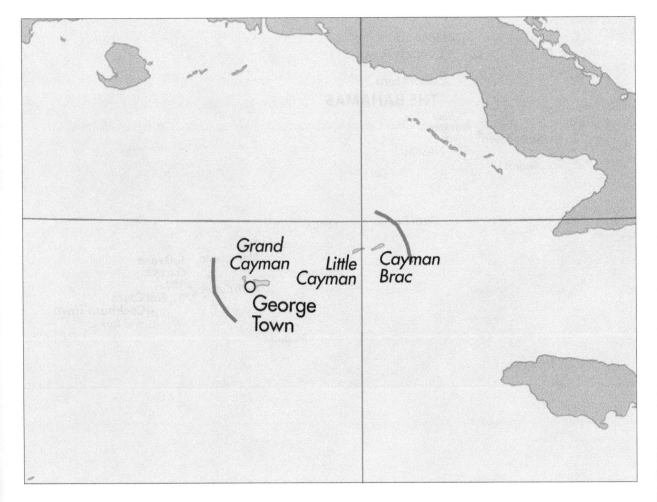

Turks and Caicos

The Turks and Caicos Islands lie southeast of Mayaguana in the Bahamas and north of Hispaniola.

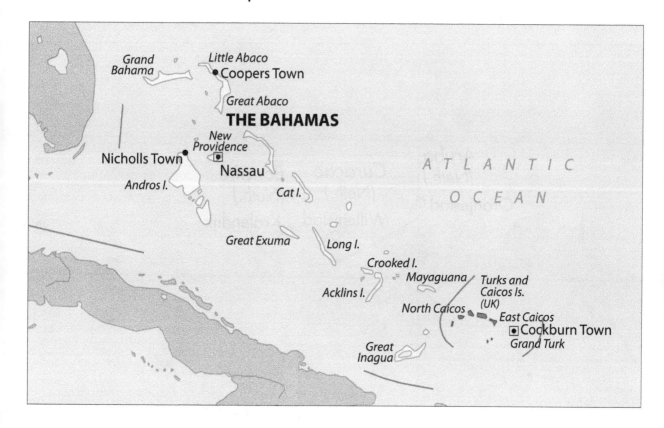

The Leeward Antilles

There are three islands in the Leeward Antilles: Aruba, Bonaire and Curaçao. They are known as the ABC islands and are located to the north of South America.

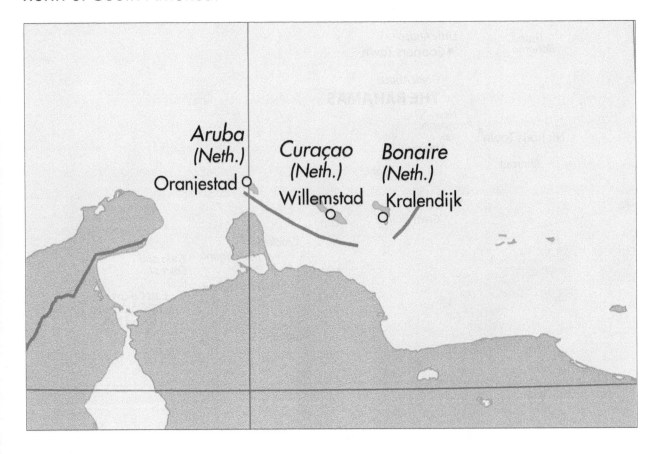

The Virgin Islands

The US and British Virgin Islands are a small group of islands located to the east of Puerto Rico. St. Croix is the largest of the US Virgin Islands.

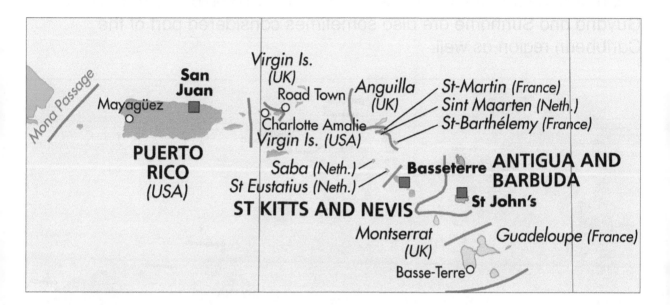

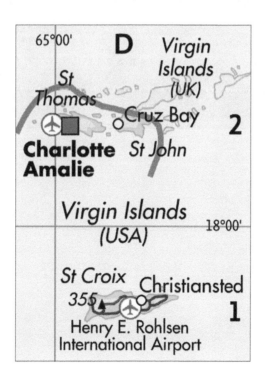

Mainland countries

The mainland countries that are in the Caribbean region are in Central and South America: Mexico (Yucatan Peninsula), Belize, Guatemala, Honduras, Nicaragua, Costa Rica, Panama, Colombia and Venezuela. Guyana and Suriname are also sometimes considered part of the Caribbean region as well.

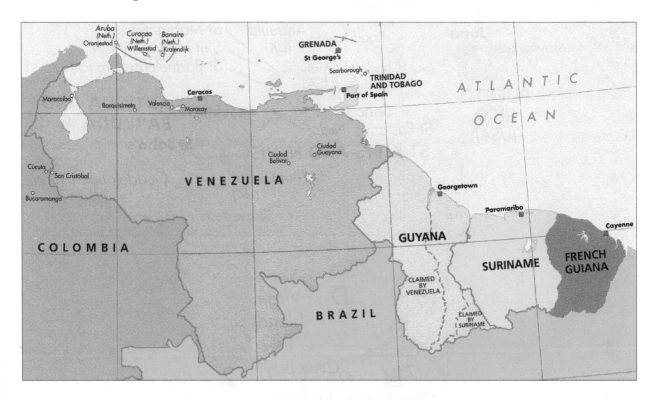

Seas and oceans of the Caribbean

The Caribbean region is surrounded by the Caribbean Sea on the western side and the Atlantic Ocean on the eastern side.

All of the Caribbean countries border the Caribbean Sea. Many of the countries also border the Atlantic Ocean.

The Caribbean Sea is one of the largest seas in the world. The water is warm, with the temperature averaging between 21 and 30 degrees Celsius during the year.

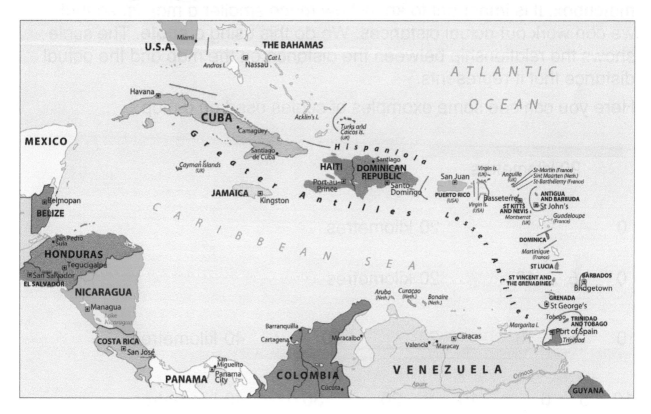

What is a map?

A map is a flat drawing of part of the Earth's surface. It may be quite small, for example, a map of a few streets in a town, or it may be much bigger and show many whole countries. A map will show the main features, so a map of an island will show the coastline, main towns and any bodies of water or high land.

Map-reading skills

Maps have their own 'language'. We need to learn this language so that we can read and understand what maps are telling us. There are certain skills that you need to learn in order to do this.

Reading and using a scale

A map of a place is drawn much smaller than the place is in real life. For example, the size of a football field may be reduced to the size of a matchbox. It is important to know how much smaller a map is, so that we can work out actual distances. We do this using a **scale**. The scale shows the relationship between the distance on the map and the actual distance that it represents.

Here you can see some examples of scales used on a map.

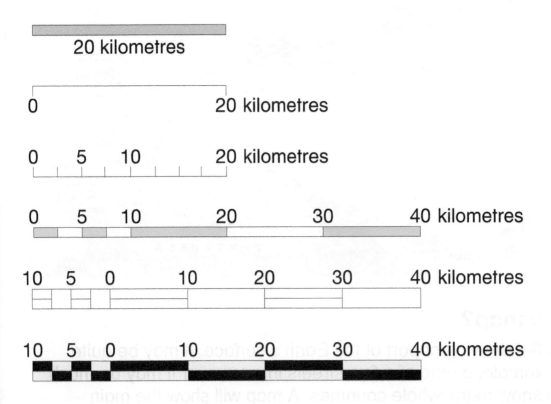

You can use a scale to measure the actual distance between two towns, for example:

- First, use a piece of paper to measure the distance between the towns on the map. Mark the two towns on the edge of the paper.
- Then place the paper along the scale, with one of the towns at zero. Read along the scale to find out the distance to the other town.

Try using the scale on this map to work out the actual distance between Potters Village and All Saints.

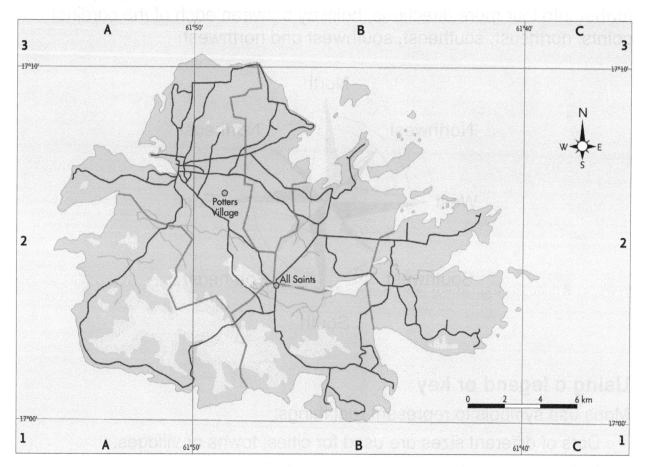

Cardinal points

Sometimes, we want to be able to say where one place is in relation to another. We do this using the points of a compass.

The main points of the compass are called **cardinal points**: north, south, east and west. These are the larger arrows on the compass below. We show north at the top, south at the bottom, west towards the left and east towards the right.

To give a direction even more accurately, we can divide the compass further into four more directions, halfway between each of the cardinal points: northeast, southeast, southwest and northwest.

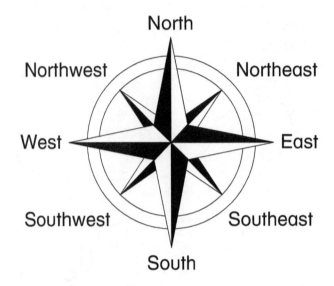

Using a legend or key

Maps use symbols to represent real things:

- Dots of different sizes are used for cities, towns or villages.
- Colours are used to show the height of the land.
- Different sorts of line are used to show coastline, roads, rivers and parish boundaries.

There may also be symbols to show things like hotels, gas stations and golf courses.

The meanings of the symbols on the map are shown on its **legend** or **key**. Look at the legend on this map of Antigua and Barbuda to help you become familiar with the different types of symbol.

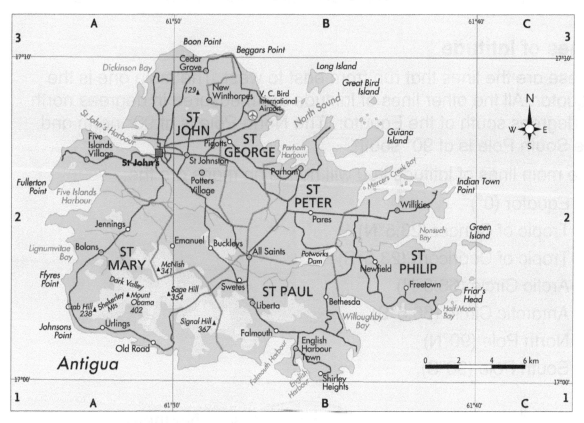

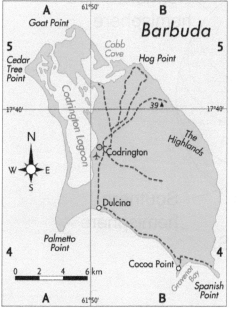

Key

	over 200 m
	100 – 200 m
	0 – 100 m
402 ▲	Mountain height (in metres)
⌒	River
—	Parish boundary
■	Capital town
◉	Important town
○	Other town
——	Main road
----	Track
✈	Main airport
⊥	Other airport

Longitude and latitude

Lines of latitude and longitude are imaginary lines found on a map or a globe. These lines help us to give the exact location of places.

Lines of latitude

These are the lines that run from east to west. The main one is the Equator. All the other lines of latitude are measured in degrees north or degrees south of the Equator. The North Pole is at 90° north and the South Pole is at 90° south.

The main lines of latitude you will notice on maps are the:

- Equator (0°)
- Tropic of Cancer (23.5°N)
- Tropic of Capricorn (23.5°S)
- Arctic Circle (66.5°N)
- Antarctic Circle (66.5°S)
- North Pole (90°N)
- South Pole (90°S).

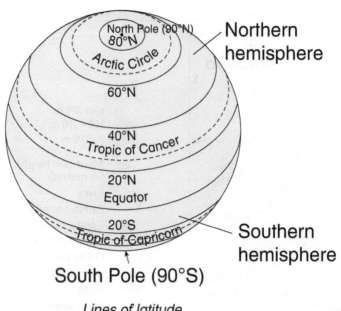

Lines of latitude

Lines of longitude

These are the imaginary lines that run from north to south on a map or globe. They are measured in degrees.

Lines of longitude meet at the poles and are also called meridians. The most important line of longitude is the Prime Meridian (also known as the Greenwich Meridian). It is at zero degrees.

Lines of longitude are measured in degrees east or west of the Prime Meridian. They help us to calculate the time in places all over the world.

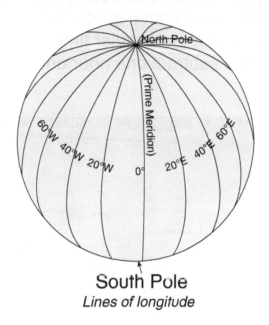

Lines of longitude

Coordinates

Where a line of latitude crosses a line of longitude, a coordinate is formed. This gives us the exact location of a place on a map or globe. Coordinates are very useful for weather forecasters who are tracking weather systems such as a hurricane, pilots who are flying from one country to another and for a ship's crew to know exactly where they are on the sea.

A coordinate is written using the degree for the line of latitude and longitude, for example, 20°N 80°E. The line of latitude is always given first.

The geographical coordinates of Antigua and Barbuda are:

- latitude of Antigua and Barbuda: 17° 03′ North of the Equator
- longitude of Antigua and Barbuda: 61° 48′ West of Greenwich.

Calculating time

Time varies around the world due to the Earth's rotation. This causes different parts of the world to be in light or darkness at any one time.

To account for this, the world is divided into 24 standard time zones and each zone is 15° intervals of longitude, which is 1 hour of time.

Each country in a zone has the same time, but time varies all around the world.

To calculate the time, you first have to identify the Prime Meridian. Places to the east of the meridian would have a later time while places to the west of the meridian would have an earlier time. For every 15 degrees west of the Prime Meridian subtract one hour and for every 15 degrees east add one hour.

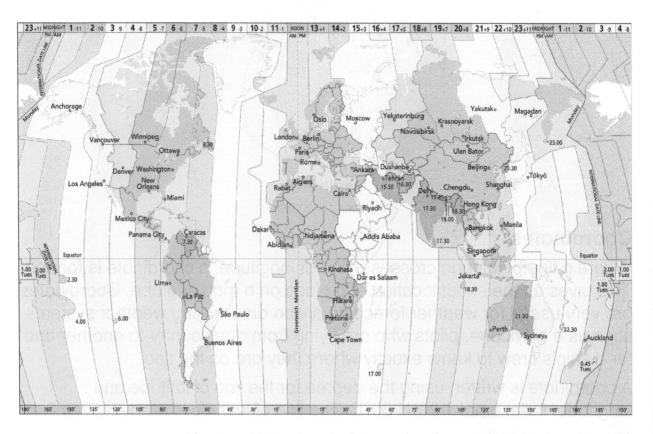

2 Parishes in Antigua and Barbuda

We are learning to:
- identify the parishes of Antigua and Barbuda on a map
- identify the size and capital of each parish
- describe the physical features of each parish and their importance to the community
- identify soil types in Antigua and Barbuda.

Parishes in Antigua and Barbuda

The island of Antigua is divided into six parishes. They are:

- St. John
- St. Mary
- St. Philip
- St. George
- St. Peter
- St. Paul.

The parishes are not equal in size. St. John is the largest and St. George is the smallest.

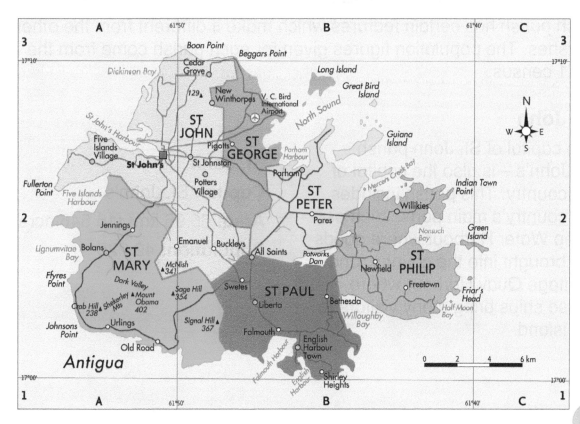

Some parishes are more densely populated than others. According to the 2011 census, over half the total population of the island live in St. John. St. Philip has the smallest population.

Barbuda is a separate island, but is run like another parish. It has the least dense population of all.

Parish capitals

Each parish has a main town, which is the capital of the parish. These towns are well provided with facilities such as a post office, fire and police stations, parks and shops, as well as the usual utilities (electricity, water, etc.). Each also has a courthouse for the Resident Magistrate and a parish church, which is usually Anglican. This is where official functions were held long ago.

Some of the parish capitals have a port, where ships come to load and unload. Others are inland. Each parish also has a number of villages.

Features of the parishes

Each parish has certain features which make it different from the other parishes. The population figures given for each parish come from the 2011 census.

St. John

The capital of St. John parish – St. John's – is also the capital of the country. This parish includes the country's main ports, such as Deep Water Harbour where goods are brought into the country, and Heritage Quay Harbour where cruise ships bring many visitors to the island.

St. John
Capital: St. John's
Area: 66.96 km² (16 546 acres)
Population: 49 225

Many of Antigua's key businesses are in St. John's, including the Antigua Public Utilities Authority (APUA), which oversees the telephone service, mobile and internet networks.

St. John's is the largest settlement in the country, with about one third of the entire population living there. Many people prefer to live in St. John's because they have quick access to the hospital, the business centres and schools. In addition, transportation is readily available to and from work.

St. John's is a popular place to live, with plenty of jobs available and good transport.

St. George

Antigua's main airport, The V. C. Bird International Airport, is in St. George and it is also home to several manufacturing companies, such as AGA Distributors, Khouly Furniture Factory, Harris Paints and Stitch World.

St. George
Capital: Pigotts
Area: 24.41 km² (6031 acres)
Population: 7496

One of the country's leading golf courses, Cedar Valley Golf Course, can be found in this parish, and there are many beautiful beaches such as Jabberwock and Shell Bay. Sea View Farm, one of the villages in St. George, is well known for its pottery.

Places of higher learning, such as the Antigua and Barbuda International Institute of Technology (ABIIT) and the American University of Antigua (AUA) are in St. George.

V. C. Bird International Airport is in St. George.

St. Mary

The parish of St. Mary, in the southwest of Antigua, is famous for its rich soil and many beaches. Many people in coastal villages such as Old Road and Urlings earn their living by fishing.

St. Mary
Capital: Bolans
Area: 63.55 km^2 (15 703 acres)
Population: 7067

The highest parts of Antigua are in St. Mary, including Shekerley and McNish Mountains, and Mount Obama, which is the highest of all.

The landscape and the soil make for lush vegetation. St. Mary produces the most mangoes in the country, and the sweetest pineapple in the world, Antigua black pineapple, is grown at Cades Bay.

For tourists, nature trails such as in Wallings Rainforest, and hotels such as Jolly Beach and Carlisle Bay, are in St. Mary.

Wallings Rainforest

St. Peter

The parish of St. Peter, in the northeast of the island, is home to historical sites such as Betty's Hope. This was the first large sugar plantation and there is now a museum there.

St. Peter
Capital: Parham
Area: 32.37 km² (7998 acres)
Population: 5269

The power from these twin windmills, at Betty's Hope, was used to crush sugar cane.

Crabs Peninsular in St. Peter is home to industries such as water desalination (removing salt from seawater) and electrical power generation. The largest dam in the country, Potworks Dam, is in St. Peter.

Many people who live in this parish earn a living from farming, and you can find much lush, green farmland. Diamond Estate, the government agricultural farm, is also located here.

St. Philip

St. Philip is the most easterly parish on the island. It gives an excellent view of the Atlantic Ocean.

St. Philip is home to one of the oldest Anglican Churches on the island, and to Devil's Bridge, which

St. Philip
Capital: Carlisle
Area: 40.67 km² (10 049 acres)
Population: 3125

is one of the main tourist attractions. Many hotels, including Verandah Resorts and Pineapple Beach, and beaches such as Long Bay, are very popular with tourists.

Devil's Bridge

St. Paul

St. Paul is home to historical sites such as Nelson's Dockyard and Shirley Heights. The parish has many beaches, for example, at Pigeon Point, and English Harbour and Falmouth Harbour are very popular for sailing.

St. Paul
Capital: English Harbour
Area: 45.27 km^2 (11 186 acres)
Population: 7979

Sailing Week, one of the country's main festivals – and popular with sailors from around the world – has English Harbour as its base. Exclusive hotels such as St. James's Club can be found in St. Paul.

View from Shirley Heights over English Harbour and Nelson's Dockyard

Soil types in Antigua

Antigua's landscape, and use of the land, is affected very much by three different types of soil. These are:

- **volcanic soil**, found in the south of the island
- **clay soil**, found in the middle of the island
- **limestone**, found on the eastern side of the island.

Barbuda has only limestone soil, as the island was formed from coral reefs.

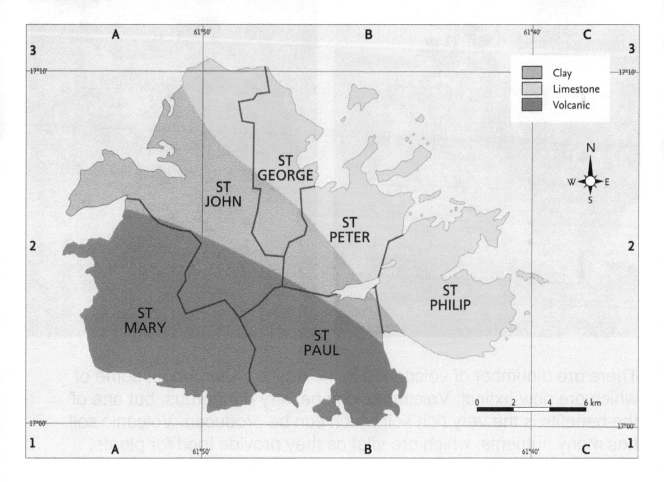

Volcanic soil

There are a number of volcanoes in the eastern Caribbean, some of which are now extinct. Volcanoes can be very dangerous, but one of the benefits is the very rich soil which can be produced. Volcanic soil has many nutrients, which are vital as they provide food for plants. This means that volcanic soil is ideal for farming.

Clay soil

Clay soil is difficult for farming because it is heavy. If there is little rain, it also becomes very hard. However, on the plus side, it is perfect for making pottery. The village of Sea View Farm is well known for its pottery.

Limestone

Limestone is used in building materials, such as cement. It can also be added to other soils to make them more fertile.

3 Settlement patterns then and now

We are learning to:

- name the indigenous people of the Caribbean and Antigua and Barbuda
- know the route taken by the early settlers
- name the ethnic groups that settled in Antigua
- name the ethnic groups in Antigua today
- describe the effect on our culture of the ethnic groups that settled in Antigua.

Indigenous people of Antigua and Barbuda

The first people who we know lived in the Caribbean were the Amerindians, who settled on the islands about 18 000 years ago. The first people known to live in a place are called its **indigenous people**.

People who settled in Antigua

A **settlement** is a place where people establish a community. The Amerindians began their very long journey from their original settlements in Siberia. Gradually, they crossed over to North America then travelled south to Central and South America.

During their movement southwards, some of the Amerindians established settlements in various places, forming indigenous tribes. Others moved further south.

This map shows the route they took.

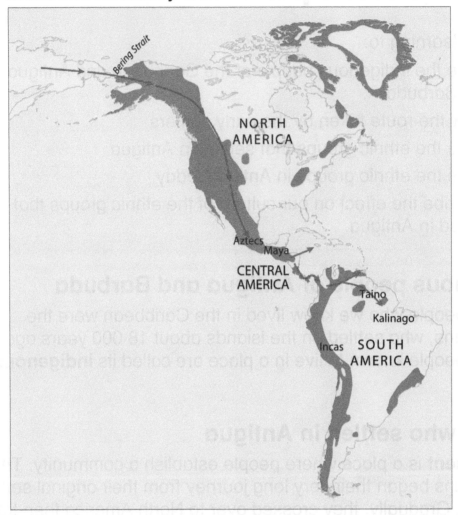

Try tracing the route of their journey on a globe. This will give you a better idea of quite how far they travelled. Altogether, the journey would probably have taken over 100 years.

The Amerindians

Between 2000 and 2500 years ago, a new group of Amerindians travelled to the Caribbean from what is now Venezuela, and began to settle in Antigua.

These were the Arawaks and the Caribs. The Caribs settled mainly in the Lesser Antilles, on islands like Grenada, Dominica, and St. Vincent and the Grenadines, as well as in the north and west of Trinidad.

The Arawaks settled mainly in the Greater Antilles, on islands like Cuba, Jamaica, Hispaniola and Tobago.

Both established their settlements along the coast, near rivers and at the top of hills. They lived in small groups. They were browned-skinned people with long straight hair. Some small groups of descendants of the Arawaks and Caribs still live in the Caribbean and South America.

The Amerindians were the first people who settled in the Caribbean. They came by canoe from South America.

The Arawaks

The Arawaks were gentle people, who shared their possessions and food with each other. The Arawak leader was called a Cacique. He made all the laws for the people and lived in the best house in the village. He wore beautiful clothes, decorated with feathers and shells. He had to be wise and strong to control the members of the group.

Here you can see what Arawak homes would have looked like.

The Arawaks lived in cone-shaped houses with thatched roofs. The walls were made of reeds and mud. There were hammocks and clay pots inside the houses, but no furniture.

They grew lots of fruits and vegetables. The men cut down and burnt trees. The women used sticks to dig holes and planted cassava and sweet potatoes. They made cassareep from the cassava juice. They used this, with peppers, and meat or fish, to make pepperpot.

The men hunted and fished. They used wooden spears, woven fish traps, shellfish tools and nets.

The Arawaks were clever with their hands. They made many things from the natural resources they found around them. They made pottery with red clay, hammocks from cotton fibres, baskets from the grass and beautifully carved trays from wood. They were also good boat builders. They used stone and shell axes to make canoes from tree trunks.

Modern-day Arawaks

They worshipped gods that lived in the world around them and the spirits of their ancestors.

The Caribs

The Caribs also lived in small groups. They were more fierce and warlike than the Arawaks.

The Carib chief was called Ouboutou. He was especially powerful in times of war. He had to be a strong warrior and he made the laws for the people. The priest was another important leader. He healed the sick with bush medicines.

The Caribs built large rectangular houses for the men and the older boys. The boys were trained to be warriors and priests. The women and children lived in small huts. In the houses, there were hammocks, a few clay pots and wooden stools.

Women grew cassava, yams, sweet potatoes and tobacco in their gardens. The men hunted and fished. The Caribs liked to eat fish. Their favourite food was cassava cooked with crab and pepper. They also liked the flesh of the agouti and the iguana.

Because they were warlike people, the Caribs were good at making weapons. They made bows and arrows. They used fish bones for the tips of their spears. They made tools like stone axes. They were also able to make large canoes.

Items like this can help us learn how our ancestors lived.

The Caribs believed in spirits, and that there are good and evil spirits. The bad spirits caused sickness and death.

The Europeans

A long time after the Amerindians settled in Antigua, came the Europeans. The first European to come to the island was Christopher Columbus in 1492.

Christopher Columbus was from Spain. He landed by accident, as he did not know that the islands even existed. He was, in fact, trying to get to India. When he got to the Caribbean he thought he had arrived in India. This is why the Caribbean islands were called the 'West Indies'.

Christopher Columbus gave Antigua the name Santa Maria La Antigua. The island still has part of that name today.

Christopher Columbus arrived in the Caribbean in 1498.

After Christopher Columbus returned to Spain and spoke about his discovery, other Europeans came. First came the Spanish, looking for gold and silver. They were followed by the British, the French and the Dutch. Some of the Europeans wanted to plant sugarcane and tobacco, while others wanted to buy and sell things.

The Spanish settlers made the Arawaks work very hard. Many died from the work and from the diseases that the Europeans brought with them. The Caribs fought with the Spanish, but only a few of them survived.

Sugarcane

The Europeans brought with them crops such as sugarcane, and animals like cattle, goats and pigs.

The Europeans fought each other for ownership of the different Caribbean islands. Those who won took over that island. This is the reason why the people in the Caribbean speak different languages. The language of the island is from the country that owned it. The British won many of the islands, which is why on many of the islands – including Antigua – the main language is English.

The Africans

While the indigenous people – the Amerindians – were becoming fewer and fewer, the Europeans needed more people to work for them in their sugar plantations.

The Europeans went to Africa and forced the people there to come to the Caribbean. Millions of Africans were taken into slavery and were shipped across the Atlantic during the 18th and 19th centuries, to work on the sugar plantations and in the sugar factories.

The Africans were captured in their towns and villages, put in chains and taken onto the slave ships across the Atlantic Ocean to the Caribbean. They were chained in rows below the deck and given little food and exercise. Many died along the way. Those who survived the journey were sold as slaves and forced to work very hard. They were not paid and were treated very badly. Slaves were the property of another person and were forced to obey them.

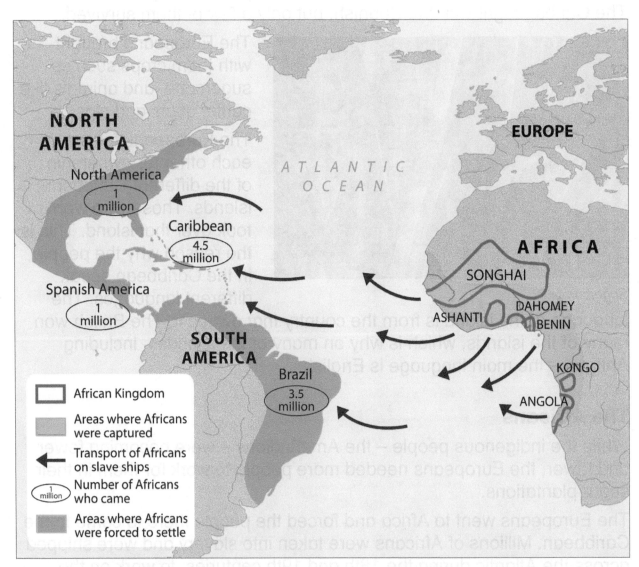

The map shows the route the slaves were forced to take, and how many of them were made to settle in different parts of America. Four and a half million were taken to the Caribbean.

Emancipation

The slave trade was a very profitable business for nearly 300 years. Slaves all over the world were treated with great cruelty.

The Africans were very strong and courageous. They fought for their freedom. Emancipation means being set free from the control of other people. The slaves in Antigua and other countries received emancipation from the British on 1 August 1834.

Today, most former British colonies in the Caribbean celebrate Emancipation Day on 1 August, or the first Monday in August.

A slave woman looking after sugar plants

The Indians and Chinese

After emancipation in 1834, many of the ex-slaves refused to continue working for the Europeans on their plantations. Instead, they left the plantations to set up their own small farms and industries.

The Europeans then turned to India in search of cheap labour. They gave the Indians a contract but paid them very little and often made them work in harsh conditions. Between 1845 and 1917, about 416 000 East Indians came to the Caribbean.

At the end of their contract, they could change their jobs. Many saved their earnings, bought land and opened shops. Some returned to their own countries but others decided to stay and make the Caribbean their permanent home. They brought their families to the islands and started their own businesses.

Many Chinese people also came to the Caribbean to work on the sugar plantations after the end of slavery, on a similar sort of contract.

This system came to an end in 1917.

Middle East

The last significant group of people who came and settled in the Caribbean came from Iraq, Syria, Palestine and Lebanon in the Middle East. This was at the beginning of the 20th century.

Most of them left their own countries in order to escape religious persecution or economic hardships. Men arrived first and used their business skills to trade goods around the islands.

Ethnic groups in Antigua and Barbuda

An ethnic group is a group of people who identify with each other based on similarities such as common language, ancestry and culture. Today, there are many different ethnic groups in Antigua.

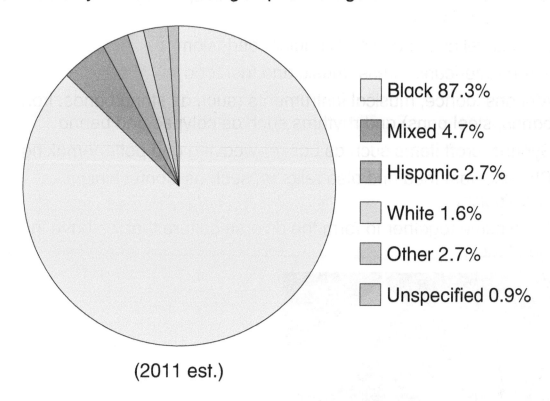

Black 87.3%

Mixed 4.7%

Hispanic 2.7%

White 1.6%

Other 2.7%

Unspecified 0.9%

(2011 est.)

We have people from all of the Caribbean islands, with the majority coming from Guyana, Dominica and Jamaica. Other ethnic groups in Antigua include the Chinese and Syrians.

Cultural legacy

All these ethnic groups have helped to shape the culture we are proud of today. Examples include:

- Europeans: languages that we speak and sporting activities such as cricket and football
- Indians: religion, such as Hinduism and Islam
- North Americans: dress, music and fast food
- Africans: dance, musical instruments (such as string bands, iron bands, steel pans) and rhythms such as calypso and benna
- Syrians: craft items such as basket-weaving and pottery-making
- Chinese: fast food and also religion, such as Confucianism and Taoism.

All these came together to form the diverse culture that we have in Antigua today.

4 The Caribbean: sustainable environment and natural features

We are learning to:

- identify natural features in Antigua and Barbuda, and in other Caribbean islands: beaches, hills, mangroves, rainforests, rivers, swamps, caves, volcanoes, hot springs, waterfalls
- describe how human activity can affect the natural environment
- identify how natural forces can change our landscape
- understand the meaning of conservation
- describe types of pollution: land, water, air, noise
- describe measures to reduce the harmful effects of pollution
- explain the causes of global warming and some of the effects in Antigua and Barbuda.

Natural features

When you look out of the window, at school or at home, you might see houses, animals, trees, ponds, hills and so on. This is our **environment** – it is everything that is all around us.

There are two types of environment, the natural landscape and the man-made landscape.

The natural environment is made up of all the features such as trees, rivers and hills, while the man-made

Most Caribbean islands have uneven coastlines similar to Antigua's, with beaches, bays, peninsulas and inlets. This beach is in Trinidad.

environment is made up of all the things created by humans, such as buildings and roads.

This chapter focuses on the natural environment.

Natural features in Antigua and Barbuda

In Antigua, we have several natural features that help to shape our landscape. These include our beaches, hills, streams, mangroves and rainforests.

Beaches

A **beach** is an area of sand or stones by the sea. Examples in Antigua and Barbuda include:

Antigua: Long Bay, Pigeon Point, Ffryes, Fort James

Barbuda: Low Bay, River Beach.

Beaches, especially if they are sandy, are very popular with tourists, so often have hotels, guest houses and restaurants nearby.

Hills

A **hill** is a high point of land which is less than 600 m above sea level. Examples in Antigua and Barbuda include:

Antigua: Mount Obama, Signal Hill, Green Castle Hill, McNish Mountain, Shekerley Mountains

Barbuda: The Highlands.

Rivers and streams

A **river** is a long stretch of fresh water that flows into the sea. Antigua and Barbuda do not have any rivers, but Antigua does have streams, which are smaller. They are:

Antigua: Ayers Creek, Cooks Creek, Fitches Creek.

Mangroves

A **mangrove** is a tree which has roots above the ground. Mangrove trees grow along coasts or on the banks of large rivers. They are one of the most common plants in Antigua and Barbuda, covering up to 3 per cent of land in Antigua and as much as 22 per cent of land in Barbuda.

Examples of mangrove areas in Antigua include:

Fitches Creek Swamp, Christian Cove, McKinnon's Salt Pond.

Rainforests

A **rainforest** is a large dense forest found in tropical areas. Examples in Antigua include Fig Tree Drive and Wallings.

Other natural features

Other natural features found in Antigua and Barbuda include:

- Lagoons, such as the Codrington Lagoon in Barbuda
- Caves, such as Bat Cave in Antigua, and Dark Cave, Indian Cave and Darby Cave in Barbuda
- Ponds, such as McKinnon's Salt Pond and Paige Pond in Antigua.

Natural features in the Caribbean

Some natural features that are not seen in Antigua and Barbuda are found in other parts of the Caribbean.

Rivers

Examples of rivers in the Caribbean include:

- Toucari River and Canefield River, Dominica
- Red River, Grenada
- Montego River, Jamaica
- Ogees River, St. Kitts
- Layou River, Dominica.

Layou River, Dominica

Swamps

A **swamp** is an area of very wet land with wild trees and plants growing in it. Examples of swamps in the Caribbean include:

- Caroni Swamp, Trinidad
- Great Salt Pond, Jamaica.

Caroni Swamp, Trinidad

Caves

A cave is a hole underground that is big enough for a person to crawl or walk into. Examples of caves in the Caribbean include:

- Goat Cave and Dropsey Bay Cave, Anguilla
- Animal Flower Cave and Harrison's Cave, Barbados
- Bat Cave, Nevis.

Harrison's Cave, Barbados

Volcanoes

A **volcano** is a mountain from which hot melted rock, gas and steam sometimes burst. Volcanoes may be:

Active: they may erupt

Inactive: they have not erupted for a long time

Extinct: they have erupted in the past but not any more.

Examples of volcanoes in the Caribbean include:

- La Grande Soufrière, Dominica
- Sulphur Springs, Saint Lucia
- Kick 'em Jenny, Grenada
- Soufrière Hills, Montserrat.

The Pitons are two old volcanic peaks in Saint Lucia.

Hot springs

A **hot spring** is a natural spring of mineral water which is at a temperature of 21°C (70°F) or above. They are found near active volcanoes. Examples in the Caribbean include:

- Sulphur Springs, Saint Lucia
- Black River Spa, Jamaica
- Ti Kwen Glo Cho and Boiling Lake, Dominica.

Volcanic Boiling Lake, Dominica

Waterfalls

A **waterfall** occurs where water runs over the edge of a steep cliff. Examples in the Caribbean include:

- Trafalgar Falls, Dominica
- Argyle Waterfall, Tobago
- Concord Falls and Victoria Falls, Grenada
- Dark View Falls, St. Vincent
- Kaieteur Falls, Guyana
- Diamond Falls, Saint Lucia.

Concord Falls, Grenada

Dark View Falls, St. Vincent

Changes to the environment

The natural environment changes all the time, with some of the changes being more noticeable than others. Changes can be caused by natural forces, such as hurricanes and earthquakes, and they can also be caused by human activity.

Look around your local area, and you can probably see some changes that may have taken place as a result of human activity. For example, where there was once an empty piece of land, there may now be houses.

Here are some examples of human activities which help to change the natural landscape of our country:

- deforestation – removing trees and other vegetation to create open spaces for human activities, or to sell timber
- excavation – digging into the earth
- farming – the growing of plants and/or rearing of animals
- building – constructing a house or factory, for example.

Mining is a way of extracting natural resources like coal, gold and tin from under the ground.

A tractor sprays farm crops with pesticide.

In Antigua, land is cleared to make room for houses and roads. Trees are cleared to make farmland. Mangrove swamps and other areas around the coastal areas are cleared for the building of new hotels. This has changed the way the landscape looks.

Forces of nature

Natural forces can also change our natural landscape. These include:

- Hurricanes – an extremely violent wind or storm. The recent category one hurricane Gonzalo caused major destruction to the landscape of Antigua in 2016 and Hurricane Irma in 2017 caused major destruction to Barbuda. Electrical wires and poles were damaged and many trees were uprooted.
- Volcanic eruptions – when volcanoes explode
- Earthquakes – a sudden shaking of the Earth
- Activities of animals.

How does the natural landscape affect the way we live?

The natural landscape affects the way people live in their different communities. For example:

- People who live near the coastal areas are most likely to make fishing their occupation.
- The shape of the land will determine how people use it – most people would choose to live in an area that is flat rather than area that has very high land.
  - Farmers would mostly prefer flat land areas to do their farming than on a hill.
  - It is better for an airport to be on a flat land area so that planes are able to take off properly.

Harming the natural environment

Changes to the landscape happen all the time. If we treat the natural environment carelessly, or wrongly, the changes to it can be very serious.

Here are some examples of how our natural environment can be misused in that way – and of the effects it can have.

- Constant mining and digging to remove natural resources like coal and tin. As well as gradually using up the resources, which are not renewable, the mining can remove good soil and vegetation.

- Deforestation – the cutting down of trees without planting replacements. This can cause soil erosion, which is when soil is washed away if it is exposed to rain and there are no tree roots to hold it together. Birds and animals can lose their habitat. Deforestation also adds to the process of global warming (see page 68).

The destruction of tropical forests can be very harmful to the planet.

- Poor farming techniques. These can really reduce the quality of the soil. Too many pesticides can harm wildlife and water quality, too.

- Removing sand from the beaches. This destroys the natural habitat for some animals.

- Cutting down mangroves and taking away corals from the beaches. This can destroy animal habitats and the breeding grounds for fish.

- Pollution – making the land, air and water dirty (See pages 64–68 for more on this.).

The following areas in Antigua are identified as 'endangered', which means they are at serious risk of being damaged.

- Nelson's Dockyard National Park
- Body Ponds
- Fig Tree Drive and Wallings
- Sugar Loaf
- Forest of Stones
- Fitches Creek
- Rendezvous Bay and Doigs Beach
- Ayers Creek and Black Ghaut Wetlands
- Rooms and Seatons Coast
- Shekerley Mountains (Mount Obama)
- hills surrounding Christian Valley.

Protecting the environment

Looking after or protecting our natural environment is called **conservation**. We have to practise conservation if we want the things in our environment to last for generations to come.

Some of the things that we can do to help the environment include:

- **Reclamation** – that means converting land that is not suitable for building on or farming into land that is suitable. One way to do this is by draining land that is very wet.

- **Afforestation** – that means planting trees to replace ones which have been cut down.

Planting new trees helps stop the effects of deforestation.

Conservation laws in Antigua and Barbuda

Here are a few examples of laws that have been passed in Antigua and Barbuda to help protect the environment.

- Trees cannot be cut down for timber within forest reserves.
- Existing forest areas may not be cleared.
- Sand should not be removed from the beaches and seashores for building or construction.
- Parts of the sea are protected as marine reserves. (See the section about coral reefs on page 71.)

Pollution

When we make the environment around us dirty, it is called **pollution**. This is one of the main ways that we can damage our environment and it is one that we can all do something about, even in our everyday lives.

There are four main types of pollution – land, water, air and noise.

All this plastic has been washed up on a beach in the Dominican Republic.

Land pollution

Land pollution is making the land around us dirty. This happens when we throw things away carelessly, or in the wrong place, causing litter. Even dropping a sweet wrapper on the ground is littering. One of the main problems comes from people throwing plastic away – when most of it can be recycled. As well as looking terrible, harmful things in the plastic endanger wildlife.

Water pollution

Water pollution is when our seas and rivers are made dirty from garbage, sewage, oil and other items. This can cause harm and sickness to the living things in the water.

This pipe is putting raw sewage into the sea. You may be able to see a slick on the water – this is caused by the raw sewage.

Air pollution

Air pollution comes from gases that humans release into the air. It causes damage to all living things that breathe them in, including plants as well as human and other animals. The main causes of air pollution are car exhaust fumes, and fumes from factories and burning garbage.

This power plant in Cuba is burning coal to make electricity.

Noise pollution

Noise pollution is a different type of pollution. It is not about making the environment dirty but about making very loud or unpleasant sounds that can damage the ears of humans and other animals. Noise pollution can be caused by planes and cars, as well as by fun activities such as jet skiing.

Airplanes bring noise pollution and also add to carbon dioxide in the atmosphere, which is one of the causes of global warming (see page 68).

Can you think of any other causes of noise pollution?

Pollution in Antigua and Barbuda

As well as problems from the careless throwing away of garbage, and other littering, there are some more serious cases of pollution. For example:

- In our capital, St. John's, untreated sewage from hotels is emptied into the sea.
- St. John's also has air pollution from all the traffic going into the city.
- Some of the factories cause air pollution.
- There is some deforestation and soil erosion.

Measures to reduce pollution

There are many ways that we can work to reduce pollution. Some of these are for individual people to follow and some are laws to make industry play their part. Here are some examples:

- People are encouraged to dump their garbage into bins where the garbage collectors can easily collect it and take it to the waste disposal.
- There is a ban on products that contain CFCs (chlorofluorocarbons). These are very harmful chemicals used in aerosol sprays, air conditioning and refrigeration systems.
- People are encouraged to use renewable energy, such as solar and wind power.
- There is an environmental tax on second-hand cars being imported into the country. This is intended to reduce the number of older cars because they will become more expensive.

Global warming

When we talk about global warming, we mean that the average temperatures on Earth are increasing. This is because some gases, including carbon dioxide and methane, trap too much heat from the sun in the Earth's atmosphere. They are known as **greenhouse gases**.

Global warming is causing changes and problems in many parts of the world. Antigua and Barbuda is no exception.

The greenhouse effect

Greenhouse gases in the Earth's atmosphere stop some of the heat from the surface from bouncing back into space. Without these gases temperatures on Earth would be around 15°C lower. This is quite normal and is what keeps the Earth a warm place to live. You can see how it works in this diagram.

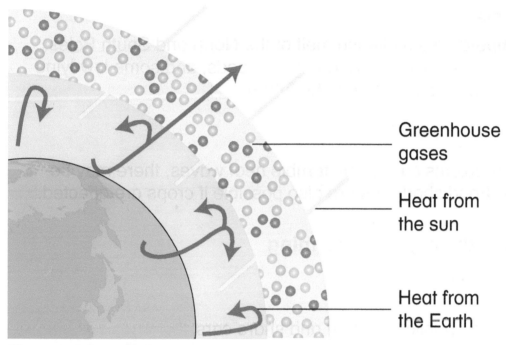

Greenhouse gases

Heat from the sun

Heat from the Earth

The greenhouse effect

The problems now are because we are producing too much of these gases, so they are building up in the atmosphere and the temperature is rising.

Here are some of the ways that the gases are produced:

- burning coal for industry and to make electricity
- using airplanes, cars and trucks, which all burn fuel
- cutting down trees, which naturally take in some of the gases.

Here are some of the effects of global warming:

Changing weather patterns (climate change)

- more powerful and dangerous hurricanes
- more droughts and wild fires
- very intense rainstorms.

Rising sea levels

The higher temperatures make ice melt at the North and South Poles. This makes sea levels rise. There are more floods, and some low-lying places may disappear altogether in the future.

Health issues

As well as the problems caused by terrible heat waves, there may be more diseases. Food shortages are also possible if crops are affected.

Measures to reduce global warming

- Plant more trees.
- Fly less.
- Drive less – use public transport and share cars.
- Recycle more to reduce waste.
- Use renewable wind and solar power.

Coral reefs

Some of the places around our islands most at risk from environmental damage are coral reefs. A coral reef is made up of coral, plants, fish and many other creatures. Over a third of all sea creatures live at least part of their lives on a coral reef.

Coral reefs are very important to life on Earth. As well as being home to many sea creatures, they are important in many other ways. They:

- provide food
- provide jobs for people who work in tourism
- produce some kinds of medicine
- protect our shores from the impact of waves and storms.

Fish feeding at a beautiful coral reef

It is important to remember that a coral reef is a living thing, so like any other living creature it can get sick and die. What is causing the damage? Here are some of the problems:

- global warming, making sea temperatures rise
- destructive fishing methods
- oil spills, plastic and other pollution
- raw sewage being sent to the sea
- chemicals from farming bringing poison as water runs into the sea
- soil from building near the coast
- careless tourism, with divers standing on the coral and anchors from boats dragging against it.

As with all the other environmental problems included in this chapter, there are things we as individuals can do to help protect our coral reefs, from not polluting the seas to supporting conservation groups and helping to educate everyone about the dangers of not protecting our planet.

5 Natural disasters

We are learning to:

- understand the difference between a natural event, a natural hazard and a disaster
- understand the causes of hurricanes, earthquakes, volcanoes, tsunamis, floods and droughts
- understand the effects of disasters on a community
- outline the role of local and regional organisations before, during and after natural disasters.

Natural events, hazards and disasters

A **natural event** is an event that normally happens without the involvement of humans. If the event would most likely have a bad effect on people or the environment, it is called a **natural hazard**. Many natural hazards are linked. For example, an earthquake can cause a tsunami and drought can lead to famine.

If a natural hazard does occur and its effects are really serious, it may be a **natural disaster**. It would certainly cost a lot in terms of money or damage to the environment but would probably also involve loss of human life.

Floods, tornados, hurricanes, volcanic eruptions, earthquakes, heat waves, tsunamis, droughts or landslides may all bring disasters.

Hurricanes

A hurricane is an extremely powerful storm that starts over warm tropical seas. It spins in the air just like a top can spin on the ground, with winds of over 119 km/hr (74 mph).

What causes a hurricane?

Hurricanes form over seas that are very warm during the summer. The heat of the water that is evaporating from the ocean is like food for the storm, making it bigger and bigger.

Hurricanes affecting the Caribbean region often start off the coast of Africa and travel right across the Atlantic Ocean to the Caribbean, picking up speed and strength. They are the only natural disaster that happens every year, though some years are much worse than others and not all of the Caribbean is affected.

The hurricane season in the Caribbean region runs from the start of June to the end of November each year.

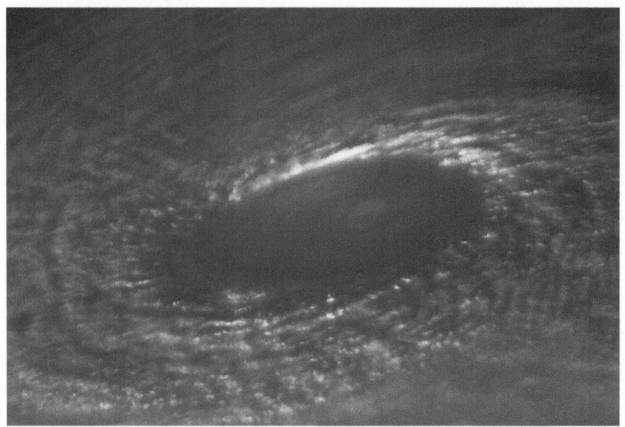

A hurricane forming over the Atlantic Ocean and heading for the Caribbean

Categories of hurricane

Hurricanes are grouped according to how powerful they are – how fast they are spinning and therefore how much damage they can do. A special scale called a Saffir–Simpson scale is used, with five categories. Category 5 has the strongest winds. Hurricane Irma in 2017 was a category 5+++ hurricane, which means it was super-powerful.

Hurricanes slowly but surely lose their strength when they travel over cooler water and over land. This happens because they are no longer getting 'food' from the warm water.

Saffir–Simpson Hurricane Scale

Category	Wind speed (mph)	Type of damage	
1	74–95	Some damage	• damage mainly to trees • no substantial damage to buildings, some damage to poorly constructed signs.
2	96–110	Extensive damage	• some trees blown down • some damage to windows, doors and roofing, but no major destruction to buildings • coastal roads cut off.
3	111–129	Devastating damage	• large trees blown down • some damage to roofing, windows and doors • some structural damage to small buildings • serious flooding along the coast.
4	130–156	Extreme damage	• shrubs, trees and all signs blown down • extensive damage to roofs, windows and doors • flooding and floating debris cause major damage to houses.
5	157 and above	Catastrophic damage	• considerable damage to roofs of buildings • very severe and extensive damage to windows and doors • complete buildings destroyed • major damage to homes.

The effects of hurricanes

A hurricane seen from a satellite above can be a beautiful thing – but it is one of the most powerful and deadliest forces in nature. The effects can include:

- loss of life and property
- a storm surge (a huge amount of water brought ashore)
- flooding
- loss of power
- damage to roads and buildings
- damage to vegetation and sea life.

How to prepare for a hurricane

Because a hurricane can cause severe damage, it is very important to be prepared. A hurricane does not sneak up without warning, so we always know how much time we have to prepare. There are things that we should do before, during and after a hurricane, to protect ourselves and our property.

Before

- Board up windows and doors, cut any overhanging branches from trees.
- Make sure important documents, such as passports and birth certificates, are somewhere safe.
- Stock up on canned foods, biscuits and drinking water.
- Have a small battery-operated radio so that you can listen to weather reports.
- Charge all mobile cellular devices.
- Have torches, candles and matches ready.
- Know the location of a shelter near you.

During

- Stay indoors during the entire time the hurricane is passing through.
- Move to a shelter if your home is damaged and you are in danger.

After

- Check for damage to property.
- Check on neighbours and friends.
- Clean up!

Earthquakes

The outside layer of the Earth is called the **crust**. It is split into seven main plates, plus many more smaller ones. These are called **tectonic plates**. There are two types – oceanic plates, which are heavier, and continental plates.

Beneath the crust is a layer of very hot liquid rocks. The tectonic plates float like rafts on top of the liquid rocks.

Where two tectonic plates meet, it is called a plate margin. There are four different types of plate margin, depending on the direction the plates are moving in:

- **Constructive (or divergent) plate margins**. This is when two plates move away from each other. Volcanic eruptions are common at constructive plate margins, because the liquid rocks can erupt through the gap.

- **Conservative (or transform) plate margins**. This is when two plates slide past each other. Earthquakes occur here as the two plates move past each other.

A constructive (or divergent) boundary marks two plates that are moving apart from each other.

A conservative (or transform) boundary occurs where two plates slide past each other.

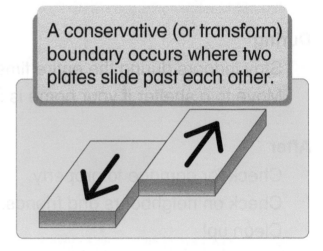

- **Destructive (or convergent) plate margins.** This is when two plates move towards each other. When they move towards each other, the oceanic crust is pushed underneath the continental crust, where it melts. Both volcanic eruptions and earthquakes are found at destructive plate margins.

- **Continental plate collision.** This is when two continental plates move towards each other. The continental crust cannot sink, so the land is pushed upwards instead and forms very high mountains.

A destructive (or convergent) boundary occurs where two plates made up of continental and oceanic crust are pushing towards each other.

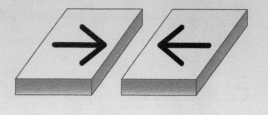

Continental plate collision occurs when two continental plates move towards each other.

The Caribbean Plate

The Caribbean Plate has four plate margins, which makes it a very active area. The North American Plate is to the north and the South American Plate is to the south. The Nazca Plate and the Cocos Plate are both to the west of the Caribbean Plate.

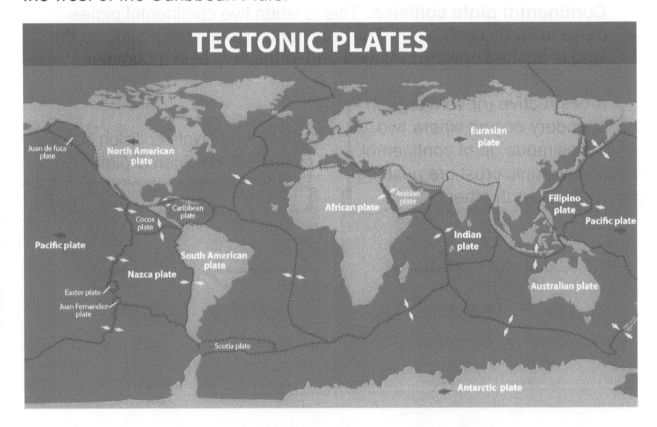

The plates are all moving in different directions and at different speeds. Sometimes the plates crash together, pull apart or slide past each other. When this happens, it often results in an earthquake.

What happens in an earthquake?

The moving plates send out shock waves that can be felt on the Earth's surface. These may be powerful enough to cause great damage to buildings, bridges and so on, and may change the surface of the Earth, with great cracks opening up. Earthquakes can also set off landslides.

The worst earthquake to affect Antigua was in October 1974. The worst earthquake to affect the entire Caribbean region was in Haiti in 2010. Over 100 000 people died.

Earthquakes happen at all plate boundaries.

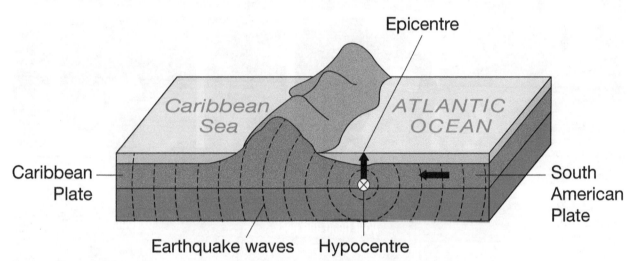

The focus, or focal point, is the point underground where an earthquake starts. The epicentre is the location on the surface of the earth directly above the focus.

What to do in an earthquake

There is no time to prepare for an earthquake as there is very little warning. The National Office of Disaster Services suggests that you: "DROP, COVER and HOLD ON".

If you are in a building, you should:

If you are outside, move away from buildings, trees, street lights and power lines, then 'Drop, Cover and Hold on' until the shaking stops.

Volcanoes

A volcano is an opening in the Earth's crust where liquid rock (known as **lava**), ash and gases may be thrown upwards. This opening is usually found in a high piece of land such as a hill or mountain.

Volcanoes are formed when the liquid rock from deep within the surface of the Earth makes its way to the surface of the Earth. This is called an eruption. As the volcano continues to erupt it will increase in size.

There are three different types of volcano:

- Active – it could erupt at any time.
- Dormant – it has not erupted in 10 000 years, but could do so again.
- Extinct – it has not erupted in the last 10 000 years and is not expected to erupt again.

Active volcanoes in the Caribbean include Soufrière Hills Volcano in Montserrat and La Grande Soufrière in Guadeloupe.

Nevis Peak in St. Kitts and Nevis has not erupted for over 100 000 years, but it is part of the chain of active volcanoes in the eastern Caribbean.

The twin peaks of the Pitons Area in Saint Lucia consists of nearly 12 square miles of land on the site of an extinct volcano.

Effects of a volcanic eruption

A volcanic eruption can cause widespread death and destruction. It can bring loss of life and property, damage to buildings, destruction of vegetation, and it can affect the climate with its huge dust clouds. The lava that flows out of a volcano destroys everything in its path.

However, unlike other natural disasters, the eruption of a volcano can have some positive effects too. These include making the soil fertile and providing scenery for tourists to visit.

Preparing for a volcanic eruption

Scientists usually have some notice that a volcano is about to erupt. They are constantly checking for any 'rumblings' beneath the Earth's surface. If that warning is given, get as far away as possible from the path the lava is likely to take. Listen to and follow all directions given by the authorities.

This house on Mount Etna in Sicily (Italy) has been buried by lava.

Tsunamis

A tsunami is a huge wave that is caused by an earthquake, volcanic eruption or landslide. They are not common in the Caribbean region, but climate change and the frequency of earthquakes have caused organisations like the National Office of Disaster Services to start educating people about the dangers of a tsunami. Schools in the Caribbean have begun practising drills on what to do in the event of a tsunami.

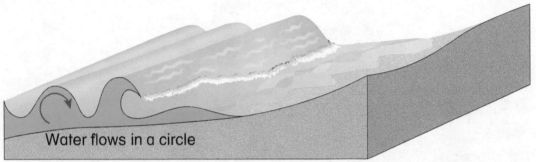

Water flows in a circle

Wind waves come and go without flooding higher areas.

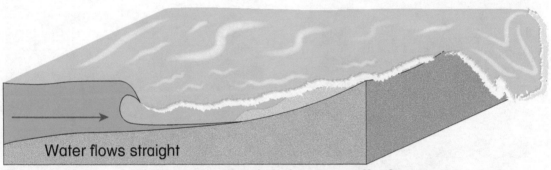

Water flows straight

Tsunamis run quickly over the land as a wall of water.

This diagram shows you the main difference between a tsunami and a normal large wave.

A tsunami can cause massive destruction to anything in its path in a short space of time. The water has enough force to kill humans and animals, destroy buildings and uproot trees in its path.

Floods

A flood is a natural disaster that occurs when there is more water than the lakes, rivers, oceans or ground can hold. It usually happens after very heavy rain that lasts for a long time, such as during a hurricane. Rivers, lakes and dams overflow, forcing the water to go onto the land. The land cannot absorb all the water so it stays on the surface.

Floods can cause severe damage to people and property. In 2016, Tropical Storm Erika brought terrible flooding to Dominica, with many deaths.

Flooding in Haiti after a hurricane in 2008

Droughts

A drought is when there is not enough water to meet the needs of the people in a country, because there has been no rain. The rivers and streams gradually dry up and the reservoirs become empty.

Humans need water more than anything else to survive. We can only last for three or four days without water to drink. Plants depend on water to survive, animals depend on the plants and we depend on both the plants and animals for food.

In recent years Antigua has suffered from a drought. This has caused the Antigua Public Utilities Authority (APUA) to introduce a water-rationing system so that water is sent to different communities at different times. This rationing makes life uncomfortable. Washing is difficult. Farmers lose money because they can't water their crops.

Local and regional organisations

There are local and regional organisations whose job is to make sure people are safe before, during and after a natural disaster. These include:

- National Office of Disaster Services, in Antigua and Barbuda
- Red Cross, across the Caribbean
- Caribbean Disaster Emergency Management Agency (CDEMA), across the Caribbean.

National Office of Disaster Services (NODS)

The role of the National Office of Disaster Services is to:

- make sure that the people in Antigua and Barbuda are aware of the possible effects of natural disasters and know how to prepare for them
- direct people where to go if they are not able to stay in their homes during a disaster such as a hurricane
- work with security personnel such as the Defence Force to rescue people in need
- help to distribute supplies to people who have been affected by a disaster.

Red Cross

The Red Cross has branches in many Caribbean countries, with local members and volunteers. Local branches work closely with governments to deliver aid. Their role is to:

- provide assistance when a disaster strikes and help supply health care, food and clothing
- make sure that the danger of illnesses is reduced as far as possible
- help in the reconstruction of buildings that have been damaged by a natural disaster
- in the case of a disaster that has caused major damage, work with regional and international Red Cross agencies
- educate people on how to prepare for natural disasters such as hurricanes.

Members of the Red Cross helping victims of the earthquake in Haiti in 2010

Caribbean Disaster Emergency Management Agency (CDEMA)

This organisation was set up to coordinate responses to natural disasters such as hurricanes, volcanoes, earthquakes and tsunamis in countries across the Caribbean region. The responsibilities of CDEMA include:

- managing and coordinating disaster relief
- getting reliable information on disasters
- reducing or eliminating the impact of disasters
- setting up and maintaining adequate disaster response.

CDEMA members include: Anguilla, Antigua and Barbuda, the Bahamas, Barbados, Belize, British Virgin Islands, Dominica, Grenada, Republic of Guyana, Haiti, Jamaica, Montserrat, St. Kitts and Nevis, Saint Lucia, St. Vincent and the Grenadines, Suriname, Trinidad and Tobago, Turks and Caicos Islands.

As citizens of the Caribbean, we must each play our part to ensure that we do everything to safeguard our own lives and property, and those of our fellow citizens, during a natural disaster.

Walkie-talkies and torches are needed in an emergency.

Sandbags help protect buildings against flooding.

6 Cottage industries

We are learning to:

- explain what a cottage industry is
- identify some types of cottage industry in Antigua and Barbuda
- explain the benefits of cottage industries
- explain the impact of technology on cottage industries
- explain what can be done to improve cottage industries
- look at examples of cottage industries in Antigua and Barbuda.

What is a cottage industry?

As the name suggests, a cottage industry is a small industry that is carried out in someone's home, often by members of the same family. There have been successful cottage industries in Antigua and Barbuda for a long time. Here are some examples:

- Making straw baskets and hats by weaving palm leaves. These were popular with tourists who visited the island.

- Making brooms from palm leaves, to be sold to local people. It was possible to stand and watch them being made.

- Further in the past, Amerindian women made pottery and jewelry in their homes and traded with others nearby through bartering.

These days, it is hard to find such hand-made items. Products such as straw baskets and hats are all made in factories. Cottage industries are still very much alive, but the products being made are quite different. In Antigua, they include:

- food items, such as jams, jellies, teabags, cake, hot sauce
- clothing and jewelry, such as dresses and beaded necklaces
- arts and crafts, such as steel pans
- hair and skin products
- leather items, such as shoes, bags and belts.

The produce is often sold on market stalls.

The benefits of cottage industries

A cottage industry is attractive to people for a number of reasons:

- A small-scale business run from home is a convenient way to start out, especially for people with small children to look after. If the business does well, it is always possible to move into a larger space at a later date.
- It is a cheaper way to start a business. There is no need to pay rent for office space or a commercial kitchen, for example.
- For customers, they know that the products they are getting are fresh and of a good quality.
- It is good for the country's economy, especially if the industry uses local resources. The small business owner spends money on raw materials to make their products. When they sell their products, the money goes back into buying more raw materials. This means that the money stays in the country rather than being spent on importing goods.

The impact of new technology

Technology has changed the way cottage industries can work. These are just a few of the ways:

- The internet can be used to advertise products. Many of the business have created Facebook pages and their own websites where their products can be displayed.
- Packaging can be more sophisticated and eye-catching in terms of design. The business can produce and print their own advertising, packaging and labels.
- Simple machines are available for packaging, for example, sealing machines that are used to seal products such as bags of fruit.

What can be done to help cottage industries?

There is much more that can be done in terms of helping cottage industries to develop. The growth of **agro-processing** is a good example of how to do this.

Take fruit and vegetables – whenever there are too many in the market, maybe pumpkins, water melons, tomatoes or mangoes, they are often left lying on the ground to rot. Agro-processing means that the food is processed to keep it fresh. This might be by making juice from it, or packaging it in a way that seals it. A small cottage business might not be able to afford the expensive machinery to do this, but with government support agro-processing can become a reality.

Examples of cottage industries in Antigua and Barbuda

Susie's Hot Sauce

Susie's Hot Sauce is a cottage industry that is known around the world. The company, which is run by Rosie McMaster, was started by Rosie's mother in the 1960s. Even today, the sauce is still made in the family house, with just a few employees to help Rosie make the hot sauce.

Susie's Hot Sauce has won awards for being one of the best sauces in the world and is a favourite of many tourists who visit the island. The varieties of hot sauce available today include five spicy and seven fruit flavours. Susie's Hot Sauce is sold locally as well as exported to countries like the USA and UK.

Zion Alternatives

Zion Alternatives is an all-natural hair and skin care line hand made in Antigua. The products made include hand-made soaps, body butters, hair grease and oils, hair gel, sugar scrubs and lip balms. They are made from natural and local ingredients.

Raw Island Products

Raw Island Products produces and sells raw organic honey, coconut oil, coconut cream, coconut butter, coconut flour, coconut wedges, coconut ice creams and coconut shavings.

7 Work and occupation

We are learning to:

- understand why people work or do not work
- consider different types of employment
- understand the benefits of employment
- identify types of worker: primary, secondary, tertiary
- understand the causes and types of unemployment
- understand the effects of unemployment on the individual, the family and the community
- understand the impact of technology on work.

What is work?

Work is when we put in some effort in order to achieve a result. It is something we all do, whether at school, at home or at other places. This chapter concentrates on what adults do in order to earn money to provide for their families.

The work or job that people do for a living is called their **occupation**. Workers get paid for the work that they do. Some are paid weekly, while others are paid monthly. Weekly pay is usually called a **wage**; monthly pay is usually called a **salary** and is often given as an annual amount.

An **employee** is a person who is employed for wages or salary, while an **employer** is a person or organisation that employs people.

Types of employment

There are two ways in which a person can be employed in Antigua and Barbuda.

Working for an employer

Working for an employer is going to work for another person or an organisation. Examples include a bank teller who works in a bank, or a cashier who works in a supermarket. These workers get a salary or wage for the work that they do.

Self-employed

Someone who is self-employed owns their own business so they work for themselves. and they pay themselves a salary from the money earned in their businesses. Examples include a farmer, a carpenter, a fisherman or a shopkeeper.

Whether they are employed or self-employed, people work in one of two sectors:

- the public sector, which is organised by the government and funded out of the taxes we pay (working in schools, for example)
- the private sector, which is all the organisations owned and run by private people.

The benefits of work

Most people who work do so for these reasons:

- to earn money so that they can provide for themselves and their family
- to have a good standard of living
- to be independent and not have to rely on others
- to provide for the future – for their retirement from work when they are older.

There are benefits for the individual, the family, and also for the community.

Individual

For the individual, as well as being independent and providing for their family, they can use the skills they are good at and their self-esteem should be better. 'Self-esteem' means how you feel about yourself – someone with better self-esteem will have more respect for themselves.

Family

For the family, adults work to be able to provide the family's basic needs. These include:

- food
- shelter (paying rent or owning a home)
- paying all the bills, such as electricity and internet
- providing food, clothing and medicine
- providing children with whatever they need for their education, such as books.

If the family's needs are met, there is a sense of comfort and security.

Community

The community benefits from the services and skills that the individual is providing. Also, workers pay taxes, which are used to provide other services for the community – roads, schools and so on.

Why some people don't work

In spite of the benefits of working, not all people do. This might be because:

- They are not able to find a suitable job.
- They do not have the right skills for a job that is available.
- They are disabled and cannot work.
- They do not want to work.

Finding work

How does a person go about finding work? There are several different ways to do this:

- look for job adverts in newspapers and on the internet
- call in to a business to ask about available jobs
- word of mouth – when friends or family hear about a job where they are working
- from electronic signs that may be posted on the roadside.

Types of work

There are three main types of work, depending on which sector of industry the job is in – primary, secondary or tertiary.

Primary workers

The primary sector involves taking raw materials from the land or sea. Workers in this sector work in agriculture (farmers), mining, oil drilling, forestry and fishing. There is a lot of primary sector work in Antigua and Barbuda.

The oil industry in Trinidad and Tobago is an example of a primary industry.

Secondary workers

Industries in the secondary sector involve taking the raw materials that were extracted by the primary workers and making them into something useful. In Antigua, many workers in the secondary sector can be found in building, manufacturing and food-processing industries.

An assembly line worker usually works in the secondary sector. This worker is checking a digital tablet on the assembly line.

Tertiary workers

The tertiary sector mostly provides services. Examples in this sector are teachers, doctors, nurses, lawyers, fire fighters, police, bankers, hotel workers, taxi drivers and mechanics. The large tourist industry in Antigua means that there are many job opportunities in the tertiary sector.

A health care worker is an example of someone who works in the tertiary sector.

Unemployment

A person is considered to be unemployed if he or she is without a paid job but is able and available to work.

Causes and types of unemployment

There are many reasons why a person may be unemployed. The time spent unemployed can be quite short or unemployment may be more long-term. Here are the main types of unemployment:

- **'Normal' unemployment:** this is when someone is unemployed because they are looking for their first job or when they leave one job to look for a better one.
- **Technological unemployment:** this happens when machines replace work that has been done by hand in the past.
- **Seasonal unemployment:** this happens when the demand for particular goods and services falls because of the time of year. For example, some industries such as tourism and agriculture lay off workers when there are no crops to pick or no tourists in the hotels.
- **Cyclical unemployment:** this is when the general economy of a country or region is poor. Unemployment also goes up then because industries are not growing.
- **Structural unemployment:** this is when an industry declines because there is less demand for what it produces. For example, in most parts of the world there is a move away from using coal because it pollutes the environment. People working in the coalmining industry may well lose their jobs. There will probably be new industries to replace coalmining, but the workers may not have the right skills.

The effects of unemployment

Being unemployed can be very difficult for a person and their family, especially if it goes on for a long time. They will have a lot less money to spend and they may not be able to afford enough good food, for example. This affects the whole family.

For the individual who is unemployed, there is also a problem of poor self-esteem and loss of confidence.

The community is affected too, as less money is being spent on goods and services.

The impact of technology

New technology is changing the way work is done. This applies to countries throughout the world, and Antigua and Barbuda is no exception. For example, the use of computers and the internet means that more and more people are working from home rather than going into separate places of work. People can even live in one country and work for a company in another country!

It is not always necessary now for people to travel out of the country to receive training for their jobs, which often used to be the case. They can do a lot of training through online e-learning courses.

The use of up-to-date machinery can help to make life easier for workers in manufacturing industries.

8 Fishing

We are learning to:
- define the terms 'fishing' and 'aquaculture'
- explain the role of fishing in the economy of Antigua and Barbuda
- name the main fishing ports in Antigua and Barbuda
- name the major fishing countries in the world
- describe fishing methods used in Antigua and Barbuda
- name imported fish products
- identify the equipment and organisation needed for fish processing
- outline the problems which affect fishing in Antigua and Barbuda.

Fishing

Fishing is the activity of catching fish, either for food or as a sport. It is the main industry for Barbuda and provides the main income for people who live around the coastal areas in Antigua.

Aquaculture is the farming of fish and other sea creatures. There are several fish farms in Antigua and Barbuda that harvest fish. One example is the Indies Green Organic Aquaponics Farm, in Sea View Farm. They rear and harvest tilapia fish.

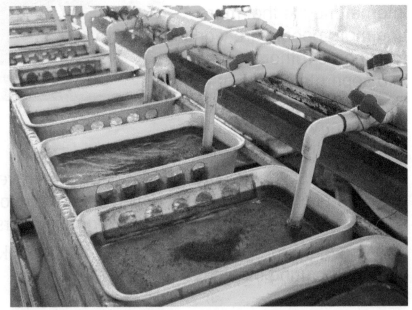

A tilapia hatchery system

The fishing industry in Antigua and Barbuda

Barbuda depends on fishing as its main industry. Fishing is also important in Antigua, especially as the tourist industry depends on it.

As well as providing employment, particularly in coastal areas, it is a reliable source of food for the local population and earns some money from exports, particularly of the Caribbean spiny lobster and the queen conch.

In Antigua and Barbuda, the fishing industry employs about 1200 people in the primary sector and about 50 people in the secondary sector (fish processing for export).

In 2010, our fishers caught 51 055 million lbs of fish, with a value of US $34.7 million.

Main fishing ports in Antigua and Barbuda

A fisher can land their catch of fish (bring them ashore) to 28 different places in Antigua and five in Barbuda. The tables below identify these sites.

Landing sites – Antigua
Primary in St John's: Point Wharf, Market Wharf, Keeling Point, High St Wharf, Dredge Bay
Primary outside St John's: Urlings, Falmouth Harbour, Jolly Harbour, Emerald Cove, English Harbour
Secondary: Parham, Shell Beach, Carlisle Bay, Morris Bay, Beachcomber, Crabbs Marina, Seatons, Willoughby Bay, Dickenson Bay
Tertiary: Mill Reef, Fitches Creek, Gaynors, Five Islands, Mamora Bay, Johnsons Point, Crab Hill, Royal Cove, Valley Church

Landing Sites – Barbuda
Primary: Codrington Wharf, Pearl Harbour
Secondary: River Wharf
Tertiary: Coco Point, Two-foot Bay

The main landing sites in Antigua are Point Wharf, Market Wharf, Keeling Point, High St Wharf, Dredge Bay in St. John's, and Urlings, Falmouth Harbour, Jolly Harbour, Emerald Cove, English Harbour in the rest of the island. Codrington Wharf and Pearl Harbour are the main landing sites in Barbuda.

Major fishing countries in the Caribbean and elsewhere

Some countries in the Caribbean have a much larger fishing industry than others. These include Barbados, Trinidad and Tobago, Antigua and Barbuda, Belize, Jamaica, Dominica, Grenada and Puerto Rico.

Major fishing countries outside the Caribbean include Japan, the USA, Canada, Iceland, Spain, Australia, Norway and New Zealand.

Fishing methods

Fishing methods used in Antigua and Barbuda include fish pots, trap fishing and gill netters.

Fish pots

This method uses a box frame covered by mesh. A bait is used to lure the fish into the box, which is then closed.

Fish pot

Trap fishing

Fish traps are a very traditional method of catching fish that are used in many countries around the world. They used to be made of wood and fibre but today are usually made of metal and chicken wire. Once the fish swims into the trap, it cannot turn around to swim out again.

The key to success with a fish trap is to position the trap in the best place.

Gill netting

Gill netting is a common fishing method for sea fishing also used around the world. It is also used in fresh water and sometimes in the mouths of rivers.

Gill nets are upright panels of netting set in a straight line. There are three methods of gill netting:

- Wedged – this is where the fish is held by the netting around the body
- Gilled – this is where the fish is held by the netting behind their gill
- Tangled – this is where other parts of the fish's body is held by the net.

The fish caught in Antigua and Barbuda

Types of fish caught in the seas around Antigua and Barbuda include:

- Caribbean spiny lobster
- snapper
- grouper and grunt
- hinds, skills, mullets
- doctors, angels, old wives
- nurses and Spanish mackerel
- queen conch.

The conch is harvested by scuba diving, mainly from the southern villages of Urlings and Old Road in Antigua.

Imported fish products

The fish caught by local fisherman cannot usually meet all the needs of the local population and so some fish products are imported into Antigua and Barbuda.

Imported fish products include:

- tuna
- red herring
- salt fish
- shad
- mackerel
- salmon
- sardines.

Exported fish products

Sometimes, however, there is more than enough fish caught to meet local needs. In that case, it may be sold off more cheaply, or it may be exported. If fish is going to be exported, and so not eaten for some time, it will need to be processed in order to keep it fresh.

Fish processing

Fish processing is done in large factories. The fish may be canned or may be frozen. You can see some examples of canned fish in the pictures on the previous page.

Canning and freezing are both excellent for keeping fish fresh but they are also both expensive and need a lot of machinery.

For fish canning, large machinery is needed to clean, remove all the bones and then shred the fish. Machinery is also needed to heat the cans before the fish is put inside, and then more machinery to seal the cans after they have been filled.

For fish freezing, huge refrigerators are needed to freeze the fish and there must be an area where the fish can be cleaned before they are frozen.

Problems affecting fishing in Antigua and Barbuda

Most of the fishing in Antigua and Barbuda is small-scale – done by local fishers using small boats. The boats have much more modern equipment these days but there are some problems that affect the industry:

- The amount of fish being caught is not controlled, so sometimes fish numbers drop. This is known as over-exploitation.
- Fishers from other countries come to fish in the seas off Antigua and Barbuda.
- Not enough is always done to preserve fish if too much has been caught – so some is just thrown away.
- The weather can have a major effect, especially when there are hurricanes.

9 Leadership

We are learning to:
- define what a leader is
- identify different styles of leadership
- identify different types of government: democracy, republic, constitutional monarchy, crown colony
- outline the role of government
- outline the role of the Prime Minister of Antigua and Barbuda.

What is a leader?

A leader is someone who directs or leads a group of people. There are leaders all around us – in schools, in our homes, in the church, and so on.

Leadership refers to the way someone leads – their style of leading. Because people are all different, their style of leadership can also be very different. A teacher is a leader in the classroom, but you probably know that they have different styles of leading.

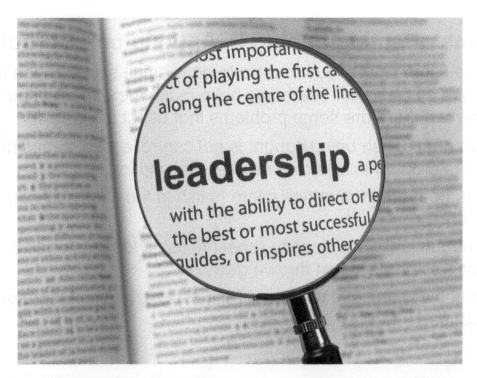

Styles of leadership

A successful leader is good at influencing people to get them to do what to do what they want. Here are some of the main ways they will try to do this:

- **Autocratic**: This type of leader is one who makes all the decisions by themselves and then tells the members of the group exactly what they should do and how they should do it.
- **Democratic:** This type of leader asks questions and has discussions with group members when a decision has to be made. The final decision is agreed by the group.
- **Laissez-faire**: This type of leader gives responsibility for decision-making to the members of the group. The leader seems to be less concerned about what is to be done or how it should be done.

What is a government?

A government is a group of people who have the power and authority to make rules to run the country. They are the leaders of the country.

Systems of government

A government is important because it provides safety and security for the people. Governments create laws and rules to protect the people. Just as there are different styles of leadership, there are different ways in which a country may be run or governed.

Gaston Browne is the Prime Minister of Antigua and Barbuda (in 2019). He is the leader of our government.

Monarchy

A monarchy is a country that is ruled by a king or queen. When the king or queen dies, the next in line – usually their child – takes over. This was the most common system of government in Europe a few hundred years ago.

Democracy

A democracy is a system of government in which a country's citizens choose their rulers by voting for them in elections. This is the type of government we have in Antigua and Barbuda.

Republic

A republic is a form of government where the head of state is not a monarch (king or queen). The government is elected by the people to rule on the behalf of all the people in that country. This type of government usually has a president as head of state.

Constitutional monarchy

A constitutional monarchy is a country that has become independent from the colonial power (a monarchy) that used to rule it. The monarch of that country acts as a head of state under the constitution. The head of state of Antigua and Barbuda is the Governor General, who is the representative of the British Queen, Elizabeth II.

Crown colony government

A crown colony government is where a country is actually ruled by the monarch of another country. Montserrat and Anguilla are currently British Overseas Territories.

Dictatorship

A dictatorship is a country which is ruled by one person who has a lot of power. They often have an army to keep that power and control the people. If they have elections, the dictator is usually the only person you can vote for.

Elections

In Antigua and Barbuda, the government is chosen by an election. This is where people cast their votes for the candidate of choice, using a ballot paper. It is a democratic process.

Democracies are countries in which all the people who can vote have an equal say in deciding who will govern the country.

After the voting is completed, the ballot papers are counted and the candidate with the most votes wins the election. The political party with the most winning candidates forms the government. The leader of that party becomes the new Prime Minister. The winning candidates take a seat in the Parliament where they become ministers and represent us as a people.

The role of the government

Our families cannot provide all the things that we need. They cannot provide us with education, health care, or a water or electricity supply. They cannot build and maintain all the roads in the country. These things are done by the government. The government is in charge of the day-to-day running of the country.

The people in the country pay taxes out of the money they earn. This money is used by the government to provide all the necessary services, such as:

- police and fire services, such as St. John's Police Station
- hospitals and health care, such as Mount St. Johns Medical Centre

- roads
- water
- telecoms
- social services (looking after people who need help in their lives)
- education services, such as the Antigua Grammar School, and teachers.

Police officers help to protect the community.

The taxes that workers pay include Education Levy, Social Security, and Medical Benefits. The government also collects taxes from other places. These include:

- property taxes
- airport taxes
- hotel taxes
- work permit fees
- ABST (Antigua and Barbuda Sales Tax)
- vehicle licences
- bar liquor licences.

Businesses also have to pay a portion of the money that they make in taxes to the government.

The Prime Minister

The Prime Minister of Antigua and Barbuda, who is the head of the government, creates ministries that help to provide these services. They appoint their ministers to be in charge of these ministries.

Each ministry is responsible for providing different services to the people in the country. For example:

- The Ministry of Education, Science and Technology is responsible for providing education from pre-school right up to university level.
- The Ministry of Health is responsible for ensuring the health care of all the people in the country.
- The Ministry of Works is responsible for roads and government buildings, making sure they are kept properly and improved where needed.

This chart shows how one of the ministries – the Ministry of Education, Science and Technology – is organised. These people are the leaders of the Ministry.

The Prime Minister of Antigua and Barbuda, who is the head of the government, creates ministries that help to provide these services. They appoint their ministers to be in charge of these ministries.

Each ministry is responsible for providing different services to the people in the country. For example:

- The Ministry of Education, Science and Technology is responsible for providing education, from pre-school right up to university level.
- The Ministry of Health is responsible for ensuring the health care of all the people in the country.
- The Ministry of Works is responsible for roads and government buildings, making sure they are kept properly and improved where needed.

This chart shows how one of the ministries – the Ministry of Education, Science and Technology – is organised. These people are the leaders of the Ministry.

Minister of Education

Permanent secretary

Assistant permanent secretary

Director of Education

Deputy Director of Education

Education officers   Curriculum officers